Grade **3**

Brain-Boosting Math Activities

More Than 50 Great Activities That Reinforce Problem Solving and Essential Math Skills

by Carolyn Brunetto

SCHOLASTIC
PROFESSIONAL **B**OOKS

NEW YORK ◆ TORONTO ◆ LONDON ◆ AUCKLAND ◆ SYDNEY

Edited by Jean Liccione

Cover design by Vincent Ceci and Jaime Lucero

Cover photograph by David S. Waitz

Interior design by Ellen Matlach Hassell for Boultinghouse & Boultinghouse, Inc.

Interior illustrations by Heidi Chang and Manuel Rivera

ISBN 0-590-06558-0

12 11 10 9 8 7 6 5 4 3 2 1   7 8 9 / 9 / 01 / 0

Contents

(continued on the next page)

✳ This activity includes a reproducible.

✳ This activity includes a reproducible.

Introduction

What is *Brain-Boosting Math Activities*?

Brain-Boosting Math Activities is a series of six books, for grades one through six. Each book contains a unique collection of activities that reinforce important grade-level mathematics concepts. We know content is important to you. So we've carefully selected activities to reinforce the most important math topics at each grade. We also know you want students to enjoy math. So we've provided high-interest and engaging activities that will involve students as active learners. Since assessing progress is important, we've supplied ideas and formats for you and students to evaluate their learning.

How can you use *Brain-Boosting Math Activities*?

When you're teaching a particular topic in your math class, just check the table of contents to locate that topic. The content is organized in a similar sequence to most third grade math textbooks. Then browse the listing of activities to find just the right one!

CONTENT AND LEARNING GOALS

What are the important math topics you need to teach in Grade 3?

Your grade 3 book is organized by nine major content strands. If you're teaching multiplication today, take a peek and see the activities available to reinforce students' learning. Each important topic has projects, games, activities, and ready-to-use reproducibles to get students started on the road to success.

What do these activities accomplish? Every activity was designed to be purposeful and to reinforce specific learning objectives. They were also designed to get students interested and excited—to encourage them to value math and to become confident mathematicians.

GROUPING

How do you organize your class for optimum learning?

Sometimes it's important for students to work together in groups or pairs, to collaborate and communicate. Sometimes they need to work independently. Activities in this book support a variety of needs, from independent to whole class work. You'll find a grouping suggestion at the beginning of each activity.

ASSESSMENT

How can you and your students assess learning?

The National Council of Teachers of Mathematics recommends a variety of approaches to assessment of the various dimensions of a child's mathematics learning. These assessment suggestions are incorporated throughout this book.

◆ ideas for group and class discussion

◆ ideas for journal writing and written response

◆ ideas for ongoing informal teacher observations

On pages 61–63, you'll also find reproducible self-assessment forms, assessment checklists, and scoring rubrics.

Remember that you can review students' self-assessment and their journals and written responses to see not only how well they're understanding concepts but also how well they express their mathematical understandings.

THE NATIONAL COUNCIL OF TEACHERS OF MATHEMATICS STANDARDS

Mathematics as Problem Solving Students are encouraged to develop, apply, and explain their problem-solving strategies. Activities promote a problem-solving approach to learning.

Mathematics as Communication Students use manipulatives, pictures and diagrams, and numerical representations to complete the activities. Activities include ideas for class discussion; many activities include a writing connection.

Mathematics as Reasoning Suggestions for the teacher in the last step of each activity are intended to serve as prompts to help students draw logical conclusions, explain and justify their thinking, and "pull it together" to make sense of the mathematics they've just used. Activities encourage students to use patterns and relationships as they work.

Mathematical Connections Activities tie to the real world, to the interests of third-grade students, and to other areas of the curriculum. The purpose of many activities is to bridge conceptual and procedural knowledge, and to bridge different topics in mathematics.

The grid below shows how the activities correlate to the other Standards for Grades K–4.

PAGE	ESTIMATION	NUMBER SENSE AND NUMERATION	CONCEPTS OF WHOLE-NUMBER OPERATIONS	WHOLE-NUMBER COMPUTATION	GEOMETRY AND SPATIAL SENSE	MEASUREMENT	STATISTICS AND PROBABILITY	FRACTIONS AND DECIMALS	PATTERNS AND RELATIONSHIPS
9	◆		◆	◆					
10/11			◆	◆					
12/13		◆	◆	◆					
14/15			◆	◆					
16/17					◆				◆
18					◆				
19/20					◆				
21/22					◆				
23/24					◆				
25/26					◆				◆
27							◆		
28/29	◆					◆			
30/31						◆			
32/33			◆	◆	◆				
34			◆	◆	◆				◆
35	◆		◆	◆	◆	◆		◆	
36/37			◆	◆					

PAGE	ESTIMATION	NUMBER SENSE AND NUMERATION	CONCEPTS OF WHOLE-NUMBER OPERATIONS	WHOLE-NUMBER COMPUTATION	GEOMETRY AND SPATIAL SENSE	MEASUREMENT	STATISTICS AND PROBABILITY	FRACTIONS AND DECIMALS	PATTERNS AND RELATIONSHIPS
38			◆	◆					
39	◆		◆	◆					
40	◆					◆			
41						◆			
42	◆					◆			
43/44	◆					◆			
45							◆		
46/47						◆	◆		
48/49							◆		◆
50/51								◆	
52/53								◆	
54/55		◆					◆		
56		◆					◆		
57/58	◆	◆	◆	◆					
59	◆	◆	◆	◆		◆	◆	◆	◆
60		◆		◆		◆		◆	◆

Any Time Is Math Time

Use these quick activities to keep students' minds on math at the beginning or end of classtime, as they are lining up to change classes, or any time you have a few minutes to fill.

1. CLASS LINEUP

When students are in a line, ask them to start at one end of the line and count backward from 100 by 5s. Now reverse and have them count from the other end of the line.

2. QUICK Q & A

Use these and other quick questions.

- Name one way that you've seen someone use math outside of school.
- Which is closest to your height: 100 millimeters, 100 centimeters, or 100 meters?
- Which is greater: ⅔ of a pizza or ¾ of a pizza?
- Close your eyes and think: How many 1's are on a clockface?
- Which would you rather have: 10 quarters or 25 dimes?
- Which is closer to today's date: April 1 or October 1?

3. MATHMA PROBLEMS

Tell students that Mathma is a creature from outer space. They can make up silly classroom math problems about Mathma. Give them a few examples to get them started:

- There were 25 books on the shelf. Mathma ate 16. How many books are left?
- What if Mathma brought 17 of her friends to join our class. How many students would we have?

4. BREAKIN' UP IS HARD TO DO

Ask students how many ways the class could break into groups of equal size. If your class size makes this impossible, what size groups can be made that will leave fewest students unassigned to a group? Try this on different days, as different numbers of students are absent.

5. TICK TOCK!

Have students look at the clock and tell you what time it will be in one hour. What time was it one hour ago?

Any Time Is Math Time

More quick activities to keep students' minds on math.

6. MONEY GUESS

Display a penny, nickel, dime, and quarter. Tell students you'll put some coins in one hand and some in the other. Do so. Then ask them to guess which hand holds the coins of greater total value. If they guess incorrectly, start again. If they guess correctly, display the coins in that hand and ask them to tell you the total value of the coins in the other hand.

7. TWENTY QUESTIONS

Tell students you're thinking of a number between 1 and 100. Ask them to guess your number in twenty questions; challenge them to ask the fewest possible questions. Remind them to use what they know about numbers, multiples of numbers, ranges of numbers, greater than and less than, etc.

8. NEXT NUMBER ADDITION

When students are in line, give a starting number. Ask students to count off by adding a given number to the start number. For example, if you begin at 13 and each student is to add 3, the first student will be 16, the next 19, the next 22, and so on.

9. NUMBER, PLEASE

Have students add the digits in their phone numbers (no pencils and paper allowed!). Whose number is greatest? Least? Do any have the same sums?

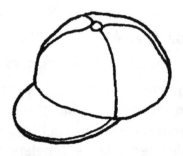

10. CLASS STATS

Use the number of students in your class on a given day to ask questions such as:

◆ How many hats for each person to wear 1?

◆ How many pens for each person to have 2?

◆ How many pieces of paper for each person to have 5?

◆ How many tables if 4 were going to sit at a table?

Fishin' With Addition

Help students "reel in" computation facts with this undersea bulletin board activity.

PREPARATION

Use colorful construction paper to cut out 16 fish shapes—10 "addend fish" and 6 "sum fish." (You may want to make the sum fish a different color from the addend fish.) Label the fish with the following numbers:

Addend fish: 1　2　3　4　5　6　7　8　9　10
Sum fish:　　15　21　25　30　39　55

Arrange the fish on a bulletin board titled "Fishin' With Addition!" Visually separate the sum fish from the addend fish—place the sum fish along the bottom of the "ocean" or jumping above the waves.

DIRECTIONS

1. Introduce the bulletin board by explaining that students will use combinations of addends to create each sum. For each sum, challenge students to use each addend only once. Do one or two examples and then show students how to record their additions. For example: $2 + 5 + 8 + 10 = 25$; $3 + 4 + 8 = 15$.

2. Challenge students to figure out which combination(s) of addend fish will create each sum fish. Make sure they record their work.

3. Change the sum fish once a week while students are practicing addition.

ASSESSMENT

As students are working on this activity, ask them to share their thought processes. Be alert for students who are using only a guess and check strategy—encourage them to try other strategies such as eliminating addends that are too large or too small, estimating sums, or quickly discarding any equation that won't work with the remaining addends.

+·+·+ VARIATION

To raise the computation level, increase all of the numbers on the fish, or change the numbers to multipliers and products.

Grouping

Individual

You'll Need

◆ Construction paper

Teaching Tip

Some students may find it helpful to draw pictures or use counters to solve the problems.

Take a Hike!

The twists and turns of these mathematical trails lead students to addition and subtraction fun!

Grouping

Individual or pairs

You'll Need

◆ Take a Hike! (reproducible page 11), one copy for each student or pair of students

Teaching Tip

Some students may need to use counters to mark their place on the trails.

DIRECTIONS

1. Invite students to "hike" math trails to add and subtract. Distribute reproducible page 11 and instruct students to "hike" each math trail from top to bottom, creating as many different answers as they can. There are only two rules—they cannot go backward on any trail (bottom to top) and they cannot use any number along a trail more than once. (16 five-number trails are possible.)

2. Discuss students' results. Record all the possible trails. Talk with students about the trails that lead to the highest numbers and to the lowest.

ASSESSMENT

Each student can assess his or her own work by "hiking" the same trails as a partner and comparing and discussing the answers.

Answers:

$10 - 3 - 4 + 6 - 9 = 0$ $10 - 3 - 4 + 6 + 9 = 18$
$10 - 3 - 4 - 3 + 4 = 4$ $10 - 3 + 8 + 7 - 5 = 17$
$10 + 5 - 2 + 10 - 13 = 10$ $10 + 5 - 2 + 10 - 5 = 18$
$10 + 5 - 2 + 7 + 4 = 24$ $10 + 5 + 8 - 3 + 9 = 29$
$10 - 3 + 8 - 3 + 9 = 21$ $10 - 3 + 8 - 3 + 4 = 16$
$10 + 5 + 8 + 7 + 4 = 34$ $10 + 5 + 8 + 7 - 5 = 25$
$10 - 3 - 4 - 3 + 9 = 9$ $10 + 5 - 2 + 7 - 5 = 15$
$10 - 3 + 8 + 7 + 4 = 26$ $10 + 5 + 8 - 3 + 4 = 24$

VARIATION

Play the game again with new copies of the reproducible. Give goal numbers and have students find the trails that will yield them. For example: Find the path that you can follow to make 34; to make 17.

Take a Hike!

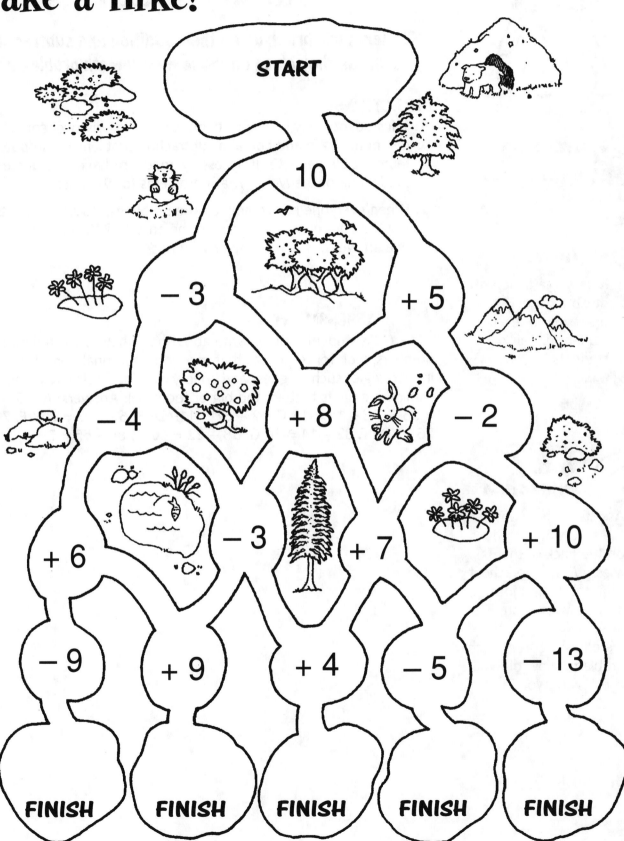

START

10

− 3

+ 5

− 4

+ 8

− 2

+ 6

− 3

+ 7

+ 10

− 9

+ 9

+ 4

− 5

− 13

FINISH   FINISH   FINISH   FINISH   FINISH

Messy Math

Students will brush up on their addition and subtraction skills as they clean up these messy math problems.

DIRECTIONS

1. Tell students they'll have to think carefully to discover some hidden numbers in addition and subtraction problems! Distribute reproducible page 13. If necessary, model or have a volunteer model one of the Messy Math problems for the class.

2. When everyone has completed the problems, discuss students' results. Does everyone agree on the answers? Was more than one answer possible? Why or why not?

ASSESSMENT

As students talk or write about how they found the missing numbers, look for responses that mention appropriate problem-solving strategies such as guess and check, working backwards, and eliminating digits that are too big or too small. **Answers: A.** 16 + 10 = 26 **B.** 28 − 14 = 14 **C.** 52 + 67 = 119 **D.** 356 − 103 = 253 **E.** 79 + 26 = 105 **F.** 32 − 14 = 18 **G.** 38 + 22 = 60 **H.** 84 − 55 = 29

Grouping

Individual or pairs

You'll Need

◆ Messy Math (reproducible page 13), one copy for each student or pair of students

◆ Pencils

Writing Connection

Ask students to answer the following questions on the back of the Messy Math worksheet or in their math journals: How did you figure out which numbers were missing from each problem? How did you check your work?

Messy Math

Oops! A messy math student spilled jelly all over these math problems! Can you figure out which numbers are hidden?

A.
```
  16
+ __
----
  26
```

B.

```
  2_
- _4
----
  14
```

C.

```
  2_
+ 6_
----
 119
```

D.

```
  _5_
- 1_3
----
 253
```

E.
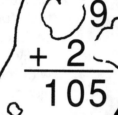
```
  9_
+ 2_
----
 105
```

F.

```
  32
- 1_
----
  18
```

G.

```
  3_
+ 22
----
  _0
```

H.
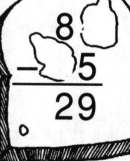
```
  8_
- _5
----
  29
```

 Make one messy addition and one messy subtraction of your own. Challenge a friend to solve them.

I.

J.

Grouping

Individual

You'll Need

For each student:

◆ Upside-Down Math (reproducible page 15)

◆ Calculator

◆ Pencil

Teaching Tip

If every student has a calculator, this activity can be done during math time. If you have just one calculator for the class to share, let students work during their free time.

Upside-Down Math

Adding and subtracting big numbers on a calculator is no problem when the answers complete a silly story.

DIRECTIONS

1. Do students know that calculators can "spell?" If students are unfamiliar with calculator "words," give them a practice problem to enter on the calculator, such as 60,000 + 17,345. When they have computed the answer (77,345), tell them to turn the calculator upside down and look in the window. The answer will appear as ShELL (SHELL).

2. Distribute reproducible page 14. Explain that students will compute addition and subtraction problems to complete words for a silly story. When students are all finished with the story, have a volunteer read it aloud.

CALCULATOR "LETTERS"	
0	O
1	I
3	E
4	H
5	S
6	G
7	L
9	G

ASSESSMENT

This activity is self-assessing; If a problem is computed incorrectly, it will not form a "word." **Answers:** ELISE, HI, GIL, HILL, GEESE, HIGH, LIE, SIGH, HISS, LOG, SOLE, SHOE, EEL, LEGS, GIGGLE, OH, ELISE, EEL, HOSE.

▶▶▶ EXTENSION

Ask students to list the "letters" that can be made on a calculator and to write a few addition or subtraction problems that result in "words."

Upside-Down Math

Read the story. Each time you come to a math problem, enter it on your calculator. Then look at the answer upside down. The answer will make a word. Write the word on the line above the problem. When you have filled in every word, read the story again!

Last week, my friend _____ came to visit. "_____, _____!"
 30,173 + 5,000 100 − 86 596 + 123

she said when she arrived. "Let's go up the _____ to see the
 8,500 − 786

_____." We headed up the _____ path until we were
29,784 + 5,555 5,000 − 386

tired. "Let's _____ down for a minute," I said with a _____.
 192 + 125 5,615 − 1,000

Just then, I heard a _____ coming from behind a
 4,014 + 1,500

_____. I looked down. Near the _____ of my
1,000 − 93 1,705 + 2,000

_____ was a big, scary _____! I turned and ran as
1,934 + 1,111 850 − 117

fast as my _____ could go. Then I heard a _____.
 2,137 + 3,500 400,000 − 23,384

"_____!" laughed _____. "That's no _____.
 21 + 19 40,000 − 4,827 400 + 333

It's just an old black _____!"
 4,738 − 1,234

Shape Search

This geometry scavenger hunt puts students on the lookout for two-dimensional and three-dimensional shapes.

DIRECTIONS

1. Tell students they'll be hunting for examples of things that are shaped like triangles, ovals, cubes, and so on. If necessary, review the following two-dimensional and three-dimensional shapes:

circle	sphere
square	cube
rectangle	rectangular prism
triangle	pyramid
oval	cylinder
trapezoid	

2. To get students "in shape" for this scavenger hunt, start them off with a few examples of two- and three-dimensional shapes. For instance, point out that a stick of chalk is in the shape of a three-dimensional cylinder, but the ends of the chalk look like two-dimensional circles. Then distribute reproducible page 17 and set students on their search. They can use the reproducible to record their findings.

3. When students return with their lists, review the shapes together. Were any found by more than one person? Were any unique? What shapes were found most often?

ASSESSMENT

Check students' findings to make sure they understand the differences between flat (two-dimensional) and solid (three-dimensional) shapes.

Grouping

Individual or small groups

You'll Need

◆ **Shape Search (reproducible page 17),** one copy for each student or group

◆ Pencils

Home Link

Have students continue the shape search at home, enlisting family members in the hunt as well.

Name_____

Shape Search

Look around your classroom or your school.
Which of these shapes can you find? Make a list
of the objects you find that have each shape.

Flat Shapes

circle

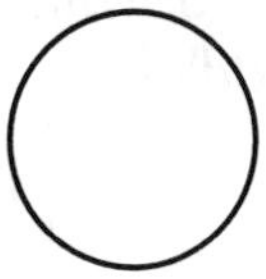

square

rectangle

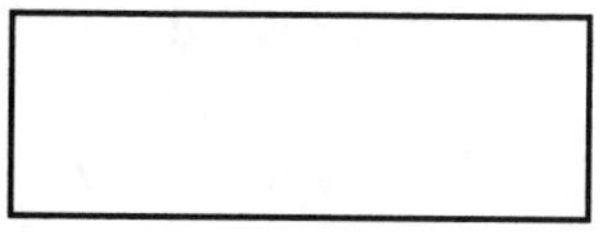

triangle

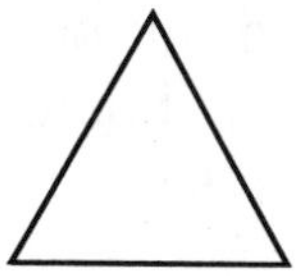

oval

trapezoid

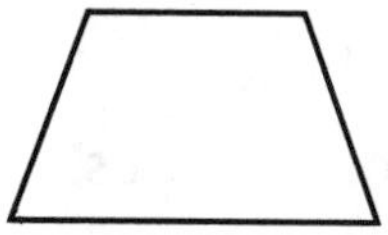

Solid Shapes

sphere

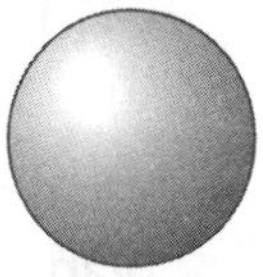

cube

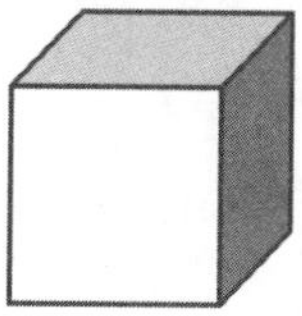

rectangular prism

pyramid

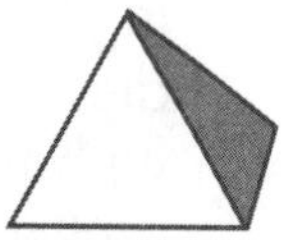

cylinder

Geometry With Riddle and Rhyme

Write me a riddle. If the riddle is fair, classmates will guess rectangle, circle, or square.

Grouping
Individual

You'll Need
◆ Paper
◆ Pencils

Teaching Tip

Help students who are having trouble getting started by having them list some of the aspects of the shape they have chosen and as many objects as they can think of that have that shape.

DIRECTIONS

1. Ask students to name as many two-dimensional shapes as they can (for example, circle, square, rectangle, triangle, hexagon, pentagon, trapezoid, parallelogram, oval, octagon). List the shapes on the chalkboard and ask volunteers to draw a picture of each shape under its name. Leave the list and the drawings on the board to serve as a reference for students' riddles

2. Read the following shape riddles aloud to students. (You may want to copy them on the board as well.)

   I have three sides.
   They might be equal, but they might not.
   Can you guess my name?

   I look like the top of a stool
   Or the face of a clock
   Or the top of a cake.
   What am I?

   Invite students to use the shapes on the chalkboard to make up their own shape riddles. Point out that a riddle may give a description of the shape, objects that look like the shape, or other clues. Encourage students to use these ideas when they write their own riddles.

3. After students have finished their riddles, hold a "geometry reading" for another class, in which each student reads his or her riddles aloud. Or display all of the riddles on a bulletin board along with the actual shapes. In their spare time, students can match riddles and shapes.

ASSESSMENT

You can get a good sense of students' grasp of geometry concepts from their riddles. Is the description of a shape accurate? Are the examples given valid? Does the writer use specific language to describe the shape?

VARIATIONS

◆ Challenge students to write poems describing shapes.
◆ Use three-dimensional as well as two-dimensional shapes.

Create a Cube

Here's a "handy" way for students to experience hands-on geometry.

DIRECTIONS

1. How does a flat piece of paper become a cube? Invite students to find out! Discuss the characteristics of a cube with your students: Is a cube a flat shape or a solid shape? How many sides does a cube have? Are all the sides the same shape? Display some shapes that are cubes and not cubes, such as blocks that are a cube and a rectangular solid. Ask students to comment on the similarities and differences.

2. After students have given their ideas, distribute reproducible page 20. Tell students they should cut out the large shape along the solid lines, fold it along the dotted lines, and place tabs with the same letter together to form a cube. You may want to have the whole class fold and tape the cubes in the same order and at the same time, following your directions.

3. Discuss the Think About It section of the reproducible. Ask students to guess what solid shape would be formed from each flat shape.

➤➤➤ EXTENSION

Ask students to bring in empty milk cartons, cereal boxes, etc. Then carefully cut or pull the cartons open at the glued areas, revealing their original flat shapes. Display the folded and unfolded cartons together on a bulletin board.

Grouping

Individual

You'll Need

◆ **Create a Cube (reproducible page 20),** one copy for each student

◆ Scissors

◆ Transparent tape

◆ Pencils

Create a Cube

Cut out the shape on the solid lines. Fold the shape along the dotted lines. Match the letters and tape the seams together to form a cube.

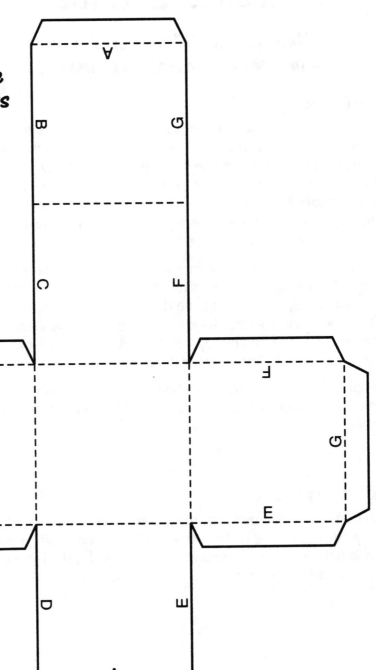

THINK ABOUT IT: What will these flat shapes look like when they are folded?

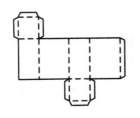
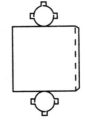
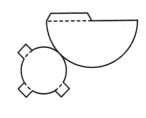

Map Mystery

Put students on the road to better map-reading skills as they follow the clues to a "mystery state."

PREPARATION
If possible, display a large map of the United States.

DIRECTIONS

1. Tell students that they'll be using directional clues to find a mystery state. Review map directions (north, south, east, west, northeast, northwest, southeast, southwest) with students. Point out some examples of directional relationships on the United States map, such as Georgia is east of Alabama or Arizona is southeast of Nevada.

2. Distribute reproducible page 22 and have students follow the directions. Point out that at each step they should follow a clue and record the state they end up in. With the last clue, they'll be in the mystery state!

ASSESSMENT
This activity is self-assessing: Students should end up in the "mystery state" of Montana. Observe interim states to be sure they're on the right track. **Answers:** Ohio, Illinois, Nebraska, Arizona, Utah, New Mexico, Montana.

Grouping
Individual

You'll Need

◆ **Map Mystery (reproducible page 22),** one copy for each student

◆ Map of the United States (optional)

◆ Pencils

Writing Connection

Have students write their own Map Mysteries and exchange them with each other.

Map Mystery

**Look at the map the United States. Use the
compass and the clues to find the mystery state!**

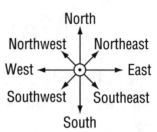

Clue 1 Begin in the state that starts
and ends with an O. You are in _____.

Clue 2 Travel two states to the west. You are in _____.

Clue 3 Travel west until you reach the state that is
one state south of South Dakota. You are in _____.

Clue 4 Travel two states to the southwest. You are in _____.

Clue 5 Travel one state to the north. You are in _____.

Clue 6 Travel one state to the southeast. You are in _____.

Clue 7 Travel three states to the north to find
the mystery state! The mystery state is _____.

Discover Coordinates!

Yo ho ho! Students set sail with coordinates as they complete a treasure map.

DIRECTIONS

1. Invite students to use a map to locate a treasure. To demonstrate map coordinates, draw a 4-by-4 grid on the chalkboard. Call out some of the letter/number coordinates that are part of the grid (the letter always comes first, as in C3) and show students how to move their fingers across rows and up columns to locate the correct squares on the grid.

2. If possible, show students some actual maps and the grid systems on them. Explain that a map index lists letter/number coordinates to show a smaller section of the map. When reading the map, that smaller section can be used to locate a given road, town, or country.

3. Distribute reproducible page 24. Have students use the coordinates to locate parts of the treasure within squares on the grid. Come together as a class to see who has found all of the treasures.

➔➔➔ EXTENSION

Give students blank 8-by-8 grids (with letters across the bottom and numbers along the left side). Have them draw their own pictures on the grids and then make a list of the coordinates on another sheet of paper. Students can exchange lists of coordinates with partners, keeping the pictures secret. Students will try to follow their partner's coordinates to draw the secret picture on another blank grid.

Grouping
Individual

You'll Need

◆ **Discover Coordinates!** (reproducible page 24), one copy for each student

◆ Crayons or markers

◆ Road maps or an atlas (optional)

◆ Pencils

Discover Coordinates!

Follow the coordinates to draw in the missing treasures on this treasure map.

C3 A jeweled crown sparkles.

B1 A ruby necklace can be found.

C5 A golden cup awaits you.

D4 "X marks the spot!"

A4 A wooden treasure chest you'll find.

E1 A silvery sword lies here.

Ant Antics

Some ants march in a line. Students can make these ants march in patterns of triangles, rectangles, and squares.

DIRECTIONS

1. Talk with students about patterns. Ask volunteers to find some in the classroom (on clothing, for example). Then distribute the counters. Give students a few minutes to come up with their own patterns using the counters. Ask each group to share their patterns.

2. Distribute reproducible page 26 and invite students to pretend the counters are ants. Tell them they'll make patterns and then draw their patterns. Work through one of the problems with students if necessary.

3. When groups have completed their patterns, have volunteers from various groups show them. This works well if you use counters on the overhead projector. Encourage the class to assess whether the solutions meet all the stated conditions.

ASSESSMENT

Observe which students are using the counters and which are able to begin to draw their ant patterns without first setting up the counters.

Grouping

Small groups

You'll Need

For each group:

◆ **Ant Antics (reproducible page 26**

◆ 24 counters of any type (beans, buttons, pennies)

◆ Crayons and paper

◆ Pencils

Teaching Tip

To make this activity even more fun, encourage students to draw their solutions in "ants" rather than in counters!

Ant Antics

Use 24 counters to stand for ants. Form the ants into
the patterns below. Draw a picture of each solution.

1. One solid rectangle, with three
equal rows of ants

2. One solid rectangle, with
four equal rows of ants

3. Two solid rectangles, each
exactly the same size

4. Six small squares, with the
same number of ants in each
square

5. One hollow rectangle, with nine
ants on each long side and five
ants on each short side

6. One hollow triangle, with
the same number of ants
on each side

7. Four small triangles, with the same
number of ants in each triangle

8. Three solid triangles—one
with three ants, one with
six ants and one with 15
ants

▶▶▶ **Make your own shape. Then describe your shape.**

Don't Wait—Tessellate!

Students will be surprised to find how easy it is to make beautiful and unique tiled patterns.

PREPARATION

Mark and cut the cardboard into 3-inch by 3-inch squares. Give one square to each student.

DIRECTIONS

Here are the steps in creating a tessellation. Demonstrate some of the process in front of the class before students begin.

1. Draw a simple shape on one side of the square. Some ideas:

2. Cut out the shape, slide it directly to the opposite side of the square (don't turn it or flip it), and tape the straight sides together.

 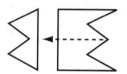 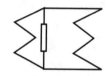

3. Repeat the process on one of the remaining sides. The tessellation template is complete.

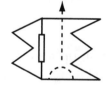 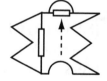

4. Trace the template in any spot on the construction paper. Slide the template in any direction (don't turn it or flip it), match the template with the first tracing, and trace it again. Repeat the process until the page is covered.

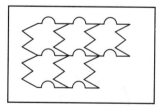

5. Color the tessellation in any way. Decorate the shapes to bring out patterns of animals, people, flowers, or designs.

➤➤➤ EXTENSION

Without a doubt, the master of the tessellation is Dutch artist M. C. Escher (1898–1972). Students might research his tessellation work, in the library or on a CD-ROM encyclopedia, and share their findings with the class.

Grouping

Individual

You'll Need

- ◆ Lightweight cardboard or oak tag
- ◆ Scissors and tape
- ◆ Crayons and construction paper (in a light shade)
- ◆ Pencils

Teaching Tip

Stop students after they have traced their tessellation templates twice on the construction paper to make sure they are tracing and connecting the shapes correctly.

Silly Stunts

This estimation game keeps students actively involved as they conceptualize lengths of time.

DIRECTIONS

1. Hold up a book students know, such as their reading or social studies text. Choose a paragraph and ask students how long they think it will take to read it. As students respond, record their estimates. Then have a volunteer actually read the paragraph, as another student acts as timer. Discuss the results. Did students overestimate or underestimate the time the reading would take?

2. Explain that you will give students a set of directions to perform a series of quick tasks. Students should first estimate how long it will take them to perform each one. After they have recorded their estimates, they can try the stunts, having their partner time them. Then they can compare the actual times to the estimated times. Distribute reproducible page 29 and have students take turns doing and recording each task.

3. After students have worked on some of the silly stunts, ask them whether their estimates were usually too long, too short, or just about right.

 VARIATION

Encourage students to think up and share their own silly stunts (within reason!) with the class.

Grouping

Pairs

You'll Need

◆ Silly Stunts (reproducible page 29), one copy for each pair

◆ A clock with a second hand that is visible to the whole class

◆ Pencils

Home Link

This activity is a great one for students to share with their families. Some of the stunts can be done in one place (at the dinner table, for example), and given that estimation can be as difficult for adults as it is for children, it's likely that parents or older siblings will be equally matched in skill with third graders!

Silly Stunts

Read each task and estimate how many seconds or minutes it will take to do it. Then try it. Record the actual time it takes.

1. How long will it take you to write all 26 letters of the alphabet?

Estimated time _____   Actual time _____

2. How long will it take you to fold a sheet of paper into eighths?

Estimated time _____   Actual time _____

3. How long will it take you to do 10 jumping jacks?

Estimated time _____   Actual time _____

4. How long will it take you to draw a square, a circle, and a triangle?

Estimated time _____   Actual time _____

5. How long will it take you to spell the word "Mississippi" out loud?

Estimated time _____   Actual time _____

6. How long will it take you to look up the word "temporal" in the dictionary?

Estimated time _____   Actual time _____

7. How long will it take you to count to 100 by 5s? By 10s?

Estimated time _____   Actual time _____ by 5s

Estimated time _____   Actual time _____ by 10s

8. How long will it take you to spell your last name backward out loud?

Estimated time _____   Actual time _____

Time for a Riddle!

Telling time is no joke—except when it helps students solve a "timely" riddle.

Grouping

Small groups or individual

You'll Need

◆ **Time for a Riddle! (reproducible page 31),** one copy for each student

◆ A variety of magazines or catalogs for cutting

◆ Scissors

◆ Pencils

Teaching Tip

Some students may find it helpful to use a play clock to form the written times under the riddle. They can then match the times on the play clock to the pictures.

DIRECTIONS

1. Use a classroom clock or demonstration clock to review telling time to the nearest five minutes. Then divide students into small groups and distribute magazines and scissors. Ask students to find and cut out pictures of watches and clocks. Have them group their cutout pictures by the time shown on each clock or watch. Then group the pictures by digital and analog styles. What generalizations can students make about how time is most commonly represented? Are certain times shown more often than others? What kind of marks show up on clock and watch faces besides numbers?

2. Tell students they'll use their knowledge about telling time to solve a timely riddle. Distribute reproducible page 31. When everyone has completed the riddle, ask a volunteer to read the answer.

ASSESSMENT

This activity is self-assessing: The letters under the clock-faces will spell the answer to the riddle when the faces are matched correctly to the written times. **Answer:** "Meet you at noon!" Look for students who are having difficulty matching the written times and analog clock faces, or who are confusing similar times (such as 3:45 and 4:45).

Time for a Riddle!

Read the riddle. To find the answer, find the clockface that matches the time written under each blank line. Then write the letter under that clockface on the blank line.

Riddle: What did the little hand on the clock say to the big hand?

Answer: "____ ____ ____ ____ ____ ____ ____
10:00   3:30   3:30   6:05   2:25   3:45   6:15

____ ____ ____ ____ ____ ____ !"
4:45   6:05   2:55   3:45   3:45   2:55

Out to Lunch

What's on the menu? Money math!

Grouping

Individual

You'll Need

◆ **Out to Lunch (reproducible page 33),** one copy for each student

◆ Play money (optional)

◆ Calculators (optional)

◆ Pencils

Teaching Tip

Some students may find it helpful to use play money or a calculator as they work through this activity.

Home Link

Ask families to let their children add up the price of their meal (or the whole family's meal) the next time they visit a restaurant.

DIRECTIONS

1. Talk with students about the prices of items in the school cafeteria or at their favorite fast-food restaurant. Discuss how much they think $5 will buy.

2. Tell students that in this activity, they'll get to "spend" $5 on lunch, choosing any combination of menu items they want! Review that when adding and subtracting money, students must align decimal points and calculate carefully. Distribute reproducible page 33 and ask students to make their choices. They should make a list of each item they want and record its price. Remind them they can't spend more than $5.

3. After students have completed their work, discuss their menu choices. Have various students read aloud their menu items; you may want another student to use a calculator to check the addition. Discuss students' choices for most healthful and most unusual lunches.

4. Have students report the total amount spent for lunch and ask them to calculate the amount of change they should receive if they pay with a $5 bill.

✛✛✛ VARIATION

Have students bring in menus from real restaurants and let them spend $10 to $20 on "dinner."

Out to Lunch

List your lunch choices on the order forms below.
Remember—you can't spend more than $5.00.

SANDWICHES AND MORE
Hamburger $1.75
   with cheese . . . . $0.10 extra
Hot Dog $1.25
Peanut Butter and Jelly $1.05
Bean Burrito $1.95
Turkey Burger $1.55
Spaghetti and Meatballs $2.15
Tuna $1.45
Grilled Cheese $1.65
Mini-Pizza $2.10

Ice Cream Sundae $2.25
Fruit Salad $1.55

SIDE ORDERS
French Fries $0.75
Potato Chips $0.45
Garden Salad $1.10
Carrot Sticks $0.65

DRINKS
Milk $0.65
Soda $0.65
Orange or Apple Juice $0.70
Lemonade $0.55

DESSERTS
Brownie $0.95
Chocolate Chip Cookies (2) . . . $0.85

ORDER FORM FOR MOST HEALTHFUL LUNCH

_____

_____

_____

_____

_____

_____

ORDER FORM FOR MOST UNUSUAL LUNCH

_____

_____

_____

_____

_____

_____

Problems and More

Put on your thinking caps to solve these problems!

1. GETTING TO 360

Write two different multiplication problems that have a product of 360.

_____

_____

2. MORE AND MORE MONEY

If you received 1¢ on March 1st, 2¢ on March 2nd, 3¢ on March 3rd, and so on for the entire month of March, how much money would you have at the end of the month?

_____

3. GOING IN CIRCLES?

Fill in the circles with the numbers from 2 to 6 so that each side of the triangle adds up to 10.

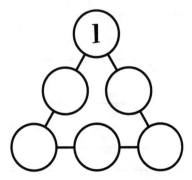

4. COIN CAPERS

How many ways can you make 50¢ using at least one penny, one nickel, one dime, and one quarter?

_____

_____

_____

_____

_____

_____

5. WHAT'S YOUR SIGN?

Fill in the missing + and – signs to make this equation true:

5 ◯ 4 ◯ 9 ◯ 3 ◯ 2 ◯ 1 = 4

Answers on page 64.

Problems and More

6. "TRI" THIS

How many triangles
are in this figure?

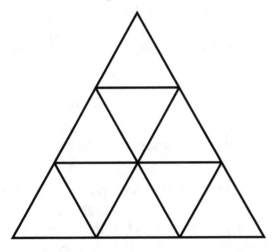

7. SHAPE TRACE

Can you trace this figure without
going over any lines?

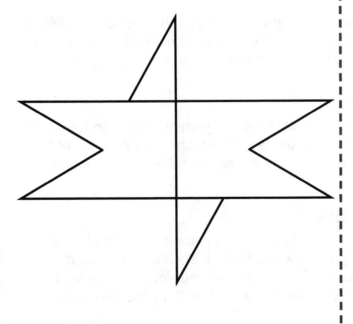

8. HIDDEN SHAPES

Find a square, diamond, triangle,
rectangle, and trapezoid in this
figure.

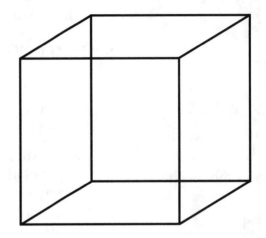

9. GIVE ME HALF

What is $\frac{1}{2}$ of $\frac{1}{2}$?
(Hint: Draw a picture!)

_____

10. TIME FOR SCHOOL

How many hours and minutes
long is your school day?

_____

Answers on page 64.

Stand Up for Multiplication

When your students play this high-energy multiplication game, the product is FUN!

Grouping
Whole class

You'll Need

◆ 18 index cards or slips of paper

◆ 2 number cubes (numbered 1 to 6)

◆ Paper

◆ Pencils

Teaching Tip

This game can get very exciting and, consequently, very noisy! You may want to add a game rule stating that anyone who calls out loses a point.

Writing Connection

Ask students to tell how playing the game helped them learn multiplication facts.

PREPARATION

Label the index cards or slips of paper with the following numbers, one per card: 1, 2, 3, 4, 5, 6, 8, 9, 10, 12, 15, 16, 18, 20, 24, 25, 30, 36. For more than eighteen players, make two sets of cards.

DIRECTIONS

1. Hand out two different number cards to each student. Explain that the numbers represent the eighteen possible products that can be created by multiplying the numbers on the faces of two number cubes.

2. Tell students you will roll two number cubes and call out a multiplication problem based on the two numbers that come up. Anyone who has a card that is the product of that multiplication problem jumps up and shows the card. If the number shown is the correct product, the student gets one point. (More than one student may have the correct product. For example, students with the 12 card may jump up for 3 x 4 or 2 x 6.) Anyone who shows the wrong product loses one point. The game ends after a specified amount of time, and the student with the most points is the winner of the day's round. Play again tomorrow, and students will have new products to watch for!

3. Students might work in groups to list all the possible multiplication facts by product to see why certain products come up more frequently than others when number cubes are rolled.

ASSESSMENT
Identify students who are not jumping up when they have the correct product, or students who are often jumping up with the wrong product. Let them work in pairs with the number cubes to get more fact practice.

▶▶▶ EXTENSION
When students are ready, increase the game to include all of the multiplication tables to 12 x 12. Make the additional product cards. Use four number cubes—roll two cubes with each hand, add the numbers on the faces of each pair, and multiply the two sums.

A-Maze-Ing Multiples!

Multiplication facts lead the way through a number maze.

DIRECTIONS

1. Do students think they can find their way through the paths of a maze? Explain to students that they will find numbers that are multiples of 4 to complete a multiple maze. Review the concept of a multiple: a number that is a product of some specified number and another number. Orally review with the class the multiples of 4, from 4 x 1 through 4 x 12. Then distribute reproducible page 38.

2. When students have completed the activity, review it together. Have volunteers read the numbers they followed in their path from Start to Finish. What generalizations can students come up with for finding the path? Is there more than one path to a solution? If numbers chosen as multiples are challenged, ask the student giving the number to verify with pictures or counters.

ASSESSMENT

This activity is self-assessing. It takes 10 steps to get from START to FINISH, and there is only one path to get there that consists of connected multiples of 4: 8, 20, 32, 28, 4, 12, 40, 48, 16, 36, 24.

 ### VARIATION

Students can make up their own multiplication mazes for multiples of other numbers.

EXTENSION

Have students make a second path that will work by changing other numbers to multiples of 4.

 Grouping
Individual

 You'll Need

◆ A-Maze-Ing Multiples! (reproducible page 38), one copy for each student
◆ Pencils

A-Maze-Ing Multiples!

How will you get from Start to Finish?
Follow only the numbers that are multiples of 4.

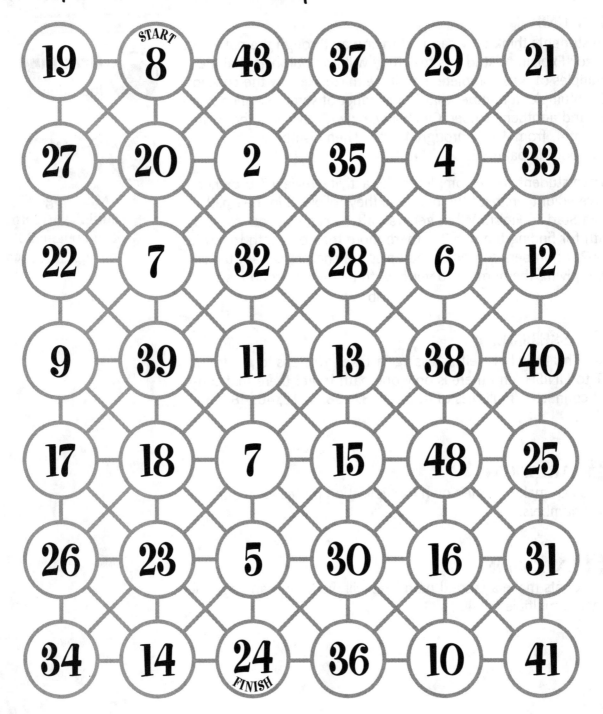

▶▶▶ On the back of your paper, tell a friend how you solved the maze.

Sailor Overboard

All hands on deck! This "runaround" game introduces students to the concept of division with remainders.

DIRECTIONS

1. In this game, you will be the "captain" and students will be the "crew." Explain that as captain, you will order the crew into "boats" of a certain number. To form a boat, the sailors line up in a row, each one resting his or her hands on the shoulders of the sailor in front. Anyone who is left out of a boat during a set of orders has "fallen overboard" and misses one round. (You may want to designate a special "overboard" area.)

2. Call out any boat size from 2 to 12. Some numbers should allow all sailors to join a boat; others should leave a remainder of sailors. For example, if you have 20 students, boat sizes of 2, 4, 5, or 10 will enable all students to be in a boat. If you call numbers such as 3, 6, 7, or 9 there will be remainders. As different numbers of sailors "fall overboard" for a round, you will be left with varying numbers of crew members and can change your orders accordingly.

3. After several rounds of play, talk with students about how the game worked. Review some of the crew sizes that allowed everyone to join a boat, and some that didn't. For a given number (such as the original total of students in the class), can students make any generalizations about the numbers that fill boats evenly and the numbers that leave remainders?

4. Show students how to represent division with remainders.

$$20 \div 3 = 6R2 \quad \text{or} \quad 3\overline{)20} \;^{6\,R2}$$

ASSESSMENT

Give some "sailor problems," such as: 16 sailors must get into 3 boats. What happens? Even if you have not yet formally taught division, ask students to write or draw a picture of each solution, including math words and symbols. The results will give you a good idea of each student's grasp of the concepts of division and remainders.

Grouping

Whole class or at least 6 players

You'll Need

◆ large open area

Teaching Tip

Play this game where students have enough space to run around, spread out, and regroup easily. You may want to set some rules such as "Any sailor pushing another walks the plank (sits out)."

Home Link

Students can play a game similar to "Sailor Overboard" at home using counters to stand for the sailors. Student and family member can take turns calling orders and arranging the counters.

Miles of Spaghetti

How far can a box of spaghetti really stretch? Students use estimation to find out!

Grouping

Small groups

You'll Need

◆ A 16-oz. box of uncooked spaghetti
◆ Pencils

Teaching Tip

If students are not able to multiply two-digit numbers, have them draw pictures at each step of the estimation process. This will help them use addition to find the total.

DIRECTIONS

1. Hold up three sticks of spaghetti end-to-end. Then place them on your desk and measure the combined length with a yardstick or meterstick. Tell students about how many inches or centimeters they stretch. Ask students how far they think all the spaghetti in the box could stretch! Tell students that they should figure out a way to find out without laying out every strand of spaghetti.

2. Divide the class into groups and give each group a portion of the spaghetti in the box. Each group will be responsible for estimating the length of the spaghetti in that portion.

3. After each group has come up with an estimate, come together as a class and add the estimates together to create a final estimate for the whole box.

4. Discuss students' estimation methods. Here are two methods students may use:

   ◆ Measure one stick of spaghetti, round to the nearest whole inch or centimeter, and multiply that number by the number of sticks.

   ◆ Measure the length of 10 spaghetti sticks, round to the nearest whole inch or centimeter. Gather the 10 sticks into a bundle and feel its diameter and weight. Then divide the remaining sticks, by feel, into bundles of about 10. Multiply the length of 10 sticks by the total number of bundles.

➔➔➔ EXTENSION

After students have estimated the total distance in inches or centimeters, challenge them to figure out what the distance would be in feet or meters. They can also try to estimate how far a line of spaghetti would extend from the door of your classroom. Would it reach the class next door? the principal's office? the playground? Students can measure and find out!

How Would You Measure Me?

This bulletin board activity lets students practice choosing the right measuring units and tools.

PREPARATION

Prepare a list of measurement words on index cards or on squares of construction paper. If you are using customary units, you could include these words: *inch, foot, yard, mile, ounce, pound, ton, liquid ounce, cup, pint, quart, gallon.* If you would like students to practice using metric units, use the following words: *millimeter, centimeter, meter, milligram, gram, kilogram, milliliter, liter.*

DIRECTIONS

1. Distribute magazines and scissors and ask students to cut out a variety of photos from the magazines, including large, small, liquid, solid, and living items (for example, animals, people, food, buildings, jewelry). Post them on a bulletin board, with a number next to each one. Then post the index cards with measurement units.

2. Ask students to determine which units of measurement they would use to measure the items in the photos. Use the bulletin board as a jumping-off point to a discussion on measurement, or have students write down their solutions. Encourage them to list more than one unit whenever possible—for example, an elephant could be measured in feet, yards, pounds, or tons!

 **ASSESSMENT**
Check that students are choosing units from the appropriate type of measurement (distance, mass, or liquid) for each photo and that they are beginning to be able to specify the most precise unit for the job (such as millimeters rather than centimeters for measuring the length of an ant).

✦✦✦ VARIATION
Relate units of measurement to measurement tools. For example, which tools would you use to measure length? weight? capacity?

 Grouping

Individual, small groups, or whole class

 You'll Need

◆ Old magazines
◆ Index cards or construction paper
◆ Scissors
◆ Pencils

 Home Link

Ask students to write down how they would measure ten different items at home.

Dinosaur Distances

Just how long were dinosaurs, anyway? Students find out by estimating dinosuar lengths in armspans.

PREPARATION

Post the following list of dinosaurs.

DINOSAUR NAMES AND APPROXIMATE LENGTHS

Name	Customary	Metric
Deinonychus	10 feet	3 meters
Stegosaurus	20 feet	6 meters
Ankylosaurus	26 feet	8 meters
Triceratops	30 feet	9 meters
Iguanodon	33 feet	10 meters
Allosaurus	36 feet	11 meters
Tyrannosaurus	45 feet	14 meters
Brachiosaurus	75 feet	23 meters
Apatosaurus	80 feet	24 meters
Diplodocus	90 feet	27 meters

DIRECTIONS

1. To get an idea of how big dinosaurs really were, ask students to estimate how many classmates, stretched arm to arm, would equal the length of each dinosaur on the list. Then have students measure each other's armspans in inches or centimeters, measuring from longest fingertip to longest fingertip. List the armspan measurements on the chalkboard and work together to round them to one unit that will be easy to work with. Each student's armspan will represent the agreed-on unit during this activity.

2. Have students line up to measure of the length of each dinosaur, touching fingertips with outstretched arms. They should "begin" each dinosaur at a common point, such as a wall or a chalk line, and count out the units aloud (for example, "four feet, eight feet..."; "one meter, two meters..."). When they have reached the closest armspan unit to the dinosaur length, mark off the distance with a piece of tape and label it with the dinosaur name.

3. When students have finished measuring out each dinosaur, compare and discuss the different lengths. Students have, in effect, created a huge bar graph!

➡➡➡ EXTENSION

For more big-number measurements, students can research the heights and weights of the dinosaurs on the list.

Grouping

Whole class

You'll Need

◆ Tape measure marked in customary or metric units

◆ Masking tape

◆ Illustrated books about dinosaurs (optional)

◆ Paper

◆ Pencils

Teaching Tips

◆ Do this activity where there is space for students to form a long line.

◆ To measure longer dinosaur lengths, mark off the longest length students can form—they can then continue measuring after the tape mark.

◆ Be sure students use one unit of measure—and stick with it.

Curves Ahead!

The world is made up of straight lines—and curves as well! This activity shows students a way to measure them.

DIRECTIONS

1. Ask students to share their experiences with measuring the length of an object. Most of their responses will probably deal with objects that have straight lines. But how would they measure something that is round or curved? After some ideas from students, explain that one way to do this is with a ruler and string. Demonstrate the process in front of the class. For example, wrap a piece of string around your wrist and mark the string where it meets. Then draw the string taut and measure it to the mark with the ruler.

2. Distribute reproducible page 44 and a ruler to each pair of students. Suggest that partners help each other place and hold the string on each of the curved shapes. Remind students that, to ensure precise measurements, not to stretch the string too much.

3. At the end of the activity, talk about the results. How accurate were students' estimates of the length of each curved line? If actual measurements are far off, have students compare procedures and remeasure the items together.

 ASSESSMENT

The actual measurements will vary somewhat, but they should be relatively close. **Answers: 1.** 14½ inches **2.** 19 inches **3.** 13½ inches **4.** 21 inches

 Grouping

Pairs

 You'll Need

For each pair:

◆ **Curves Ahead! (reproducible page 44)**

◆ Rulers

◆ String or yarn, 1 yard long

◆ Pencils

 Home Link

Instruct each student to measure one round or curved object at home. You might assign the same object to everyone in the class.

Writing Connection

Ask students to write about a real or invented job that might include measuring round or curved objects.

Name _____

Curves Ahead!

How long is each curved line?
Guess. Then check by measuring.

1. My guess _____

Actual length _____

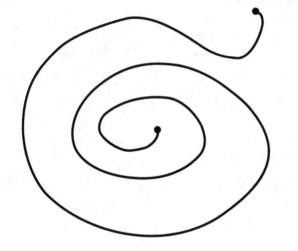

2. My guess _____

Actual length _____

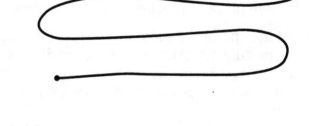

3. My guess _____

Actual length _____

4. My guess _____

Actual length _____

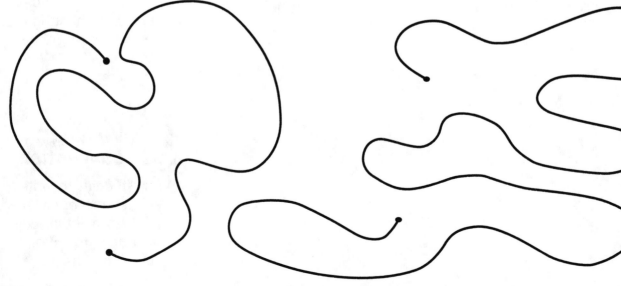

Data and Graphing

Picturing Pizza

**Which pizza topping is tops with students?
A pictograph will help them find out!**

PREPARATION
Tape the poster paper to a wall or tack it to a bulletin board. Hang the paper low enough that students will be able to draw on it.

DIRECTIONS
1. Explain to students that they will be making a pictograph showing their favorite pizza toppings. Each symbol will stand for one student's vote. First decide which pizza toppings will be shown. Ask students to offer topping suggestions and list them on the chalkboard. Keep the list to about ten possibilities, which may include "no topping," "other," and "I don't like pizza."

2. Choose a student to list the choices on the left side of the poster paper. Ask class members to come up with a title for the pictograph (such as "Room 410's Favorite Pizza Toppings") and add it to the pictograph.

3. To fill in the pictograph, hold a class poll. Remind students that they may vote only once! Call out the first topping choice and count the votes it receives. Choose a student to draw the same number of symbols after the topping as the number of votes it received. (It's best to use a simple symbol such as a happy face or a stick figure). Repeat the process for each choice.

4. Talk with students about the results. Ask questions that require students to interpret the information. For example: How many people prefer meat toppings? How many more people prefer mushrooms than sausage?

➤➤➤ EXTENSIONS
◆ Working as a class, turn the information on your pictograph into a bar graph. Discuss the differences. When is one type of graph better than the other?

◆ Ask another third-grade class to make a count using the same topping choices. Graph the results. How does your class compare with another third grade?

◆ Show students how to use a symbol to represent two students' choices. How might this technique be useful in graphing large numbers?

Grouping
Whole class

You'll Need

◆ 1 sheet of poster paper
◆ Markers or crayons
◆ Pencils

Teaching Tip

Stick-on notes are a handy way to record information. Draw your graph symbol on each stick-on note, and students can place the notes on the graph as they vote.

Home Link

Ask students to take a pizza topping poll at home and draw the results as a pictograph.

Grouping

Individual

You'll Need

◆ **Schedule Time! reproducible (page 47),** one copy for each student

◆ Pencils

Teaching Tip

You may want to have students complete their personal schedules at home, with a family member's help, and then bring them back to class.

Schedule Time!

There's no time like the present for students to learn to make a schedule!

DIRECTIONS

1. Talk with students about schedules they are familiar with. If possible, show some examples of schedules, such as a bus schedule, a TV schedule, or the like. Ask students to suggest how these schedules are useful to people.

2. On the chalkboard, draw a schedule similar to the one shown. Work with students to fill in the schedule with your own weekly class timetable (follow Monday's example). Point out that some classes start or end at a time that is not exactly on

	Monday	Tuesday	Wednesday	Thursday
8:00 am				
9:00 am	homeroom			
10:00 am	science			
11:00 am	math			
12:00 pm				
1:00 pm	lunch			
2:00 pm	gym			
3:00 pm	language arts			
4:00 pm	go home			
5:00 pm				

the hour; therefore, you will need to draw some extra lines on the schedule. Then invite students to follow the same process as they fill in their personal schedules on reproducible page 47.

3. After they have finished filling in their schedules, ask students: How does a schedule help us organize the information we need to know about our time?

ASSESSMENT

Check students' schedules to make sure they are reasonably accurate in drawing any lines between whole hours in the correct places. For example, half hours should be marked about halfway between two hours, quarter hours should be marked about a quarter of the way before or past a whole hour, and so on.

➔➔➔ EXTENSION

Ask students to bring in a train or bus schedule, a professional sports team schedule, or any other kind of real-life schedule they can find. Hang them up in your math center along with some questions.

Name _____

Data and Graphing

Schedule Time!

Fill in the schedule below with your weekly activities. Remember: some of your activities may fall between two times listed on the schedule.

	Monday	Tuesday	Wednesday	Thursday	Friday	Saturday	Sunday
8:00 am							
9:00 am							
10:00 am							
11:00 am							
12:00 pm							
1:00 pm							
2:00 pm							
3:00 pm							
4:00 pm							
5:00 pm							
6:00 pm							
7:00 pm							
8:00 pm							
9:00 pm							
10:00 pm							

Weather Watchers

"Weather" the forecast calls for rain, or snow, or sun, making a double line graph is twice the fun!

Grouping

Individual

You'll Need

◆ **Weather Watchers (reproducible page 49),** one copy for each student

◆ The weather page from five consecutive daily newspapers

◆ Two different-color-markers, crayons, or colored pencils for each student

Teaching Tip

You may want to watch the weather for a week and complete a "Weather Watchers" double line graph with the whole class first. Students can then use it as a model as they complete their own graphs for a second week.

PREPARATION

Students will need to look at the weather page of your local newspaper on each of the five days that they work on their graphs. You may want to remove the weather page from the newspaper each morning and hang it up where everyone can refer to it easily.

DIRECTIONS

1. Hold up the current weather page and discuss its features with your class. Explain that students will be keeping track of the high temperatures in two different cities for one week. Let them look at the list of cities and choose two—local, national, or international, but preferably located far away from each other. You might want to help students locate their cities on a map.

2. Distribute reproducible page 49. Have students choose a color for each city and complete the Key. They can then mark the high temperatures on the Day One column on their line graphs, using a different-color dot for each city. On Day Two, students will again mark the high temperatures in the two cities with dots and connect the dots with lines (being careful to continue the same color for each city). Repeat for Days Three, Four, and Five.

3. At the end of the five days, discuss students' results. What do the line graphs show? How is a double line graph useful in showing comparative data? Ask students to speculate as to how the graphs will look over time.

ASSESSMENT

Take a look at the lines on students' graphs. Over five days, the temperature in any city will not fluctuate too wildly—if you see any jagged lines, a student may have recorded a temperature incorrectly or transposed the two cities' temperatures.

➔➔➔ EXTENSION

Students have now recorded the weather in two cities for one week. What's the weather like in those places during the rest of the year? Have them find out, using encyclopedias, almanacs, or the Internet.

Weather Watchers

Choose two cities. Find their high temperature every day for five days. Mark the temperature on the graph and connect the marks with lines. Use a different color for each city.

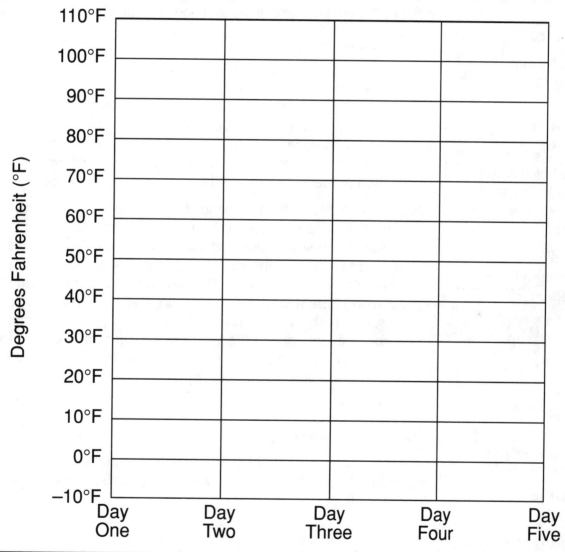

KEY

(color) = _____ (city)

(color) = _____ (city)

Goody for Fractions!

Help your students develop a taste for fractions with a delicious no-bake recipe.

Grouping

Small groups

You'll Need

- ◆ **Goody for Fractions!** (reproducible page 51), one for each student

For each group:

- ◆ Recipe ingredients (see reproducible)
- ◆ Clear glass or plastic measuring cup
- ◆ Large bowl
- ◆ Mixing spoon
- ◆ Wax paper

Home Link

Ask students to bring in a favorite recipe from home. Have students rewrite each of the fractions with a picture rather than the symbol given in the recipe.

PREPARATION

Set out the cookie ingredients and cooking supplies on a large surface.

DIRECTIONS

1. Fractions to eat? Here they are! Help students form groups so you have as many as your supplies allow. Distribute reproducible page 51 and review the recipe. Ask students to "read" the fraction picture in front of each of the ingredients and write each fraction numerically next to the pictorial representation.

2. Have students wash their hands before beginning the activity. Distribute recipe ingredients and equipment to each group. To prepare the peanut butter–oatmeal drops, you and students simply need to mix the ingredients together, roll the dough into balls, and place the balls on the wax paper. You may want to appoint different students to measure and pour in the ingredients, to mix the ingredients, and to roll the dough into balls. Encourage everyone in the group to remain seated except for the student whose turn it is to measure or stir. Then chill the finished drops for about an hour, and enjoy!

ASSESSMENT

Students should be able to relate pictorial and numerical representations of fractions. **Answers: 1.** $\frac{3}{6}$ **2.** $\frac{2}{4}$ **3.** $\frac{3}{8}$ **4.** $\frac{2}{3}$ **5.** $\frac{3}{4}$ **6.** $\frac{4}{5}$ **7.** $\frac{5}{6}$ **8.** $\frac{5}{8}$

Goody for Fractions!

NO-BAKE PEANUT BUTTER–OATMEAL DROPS

(makes about 30 1-inch drops)

⬤ cup peanut butter (smooth or crunchy)

◑ cup corn syrup

◔ cup confectioner's sugar

⊕ cup powdered milk

◓ cup uncooked oatmeal

Mix all the ingredients together. Roll into balls.
Chill for about one hour. Then eat!

**Now try these fraction pictures.
Can you write the fraction each picture shows?**

1.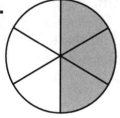

_____

2.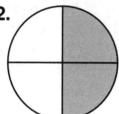

_____

3.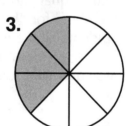

_____

4.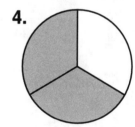

_____

5.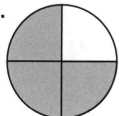

_____

6.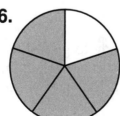

_____

7.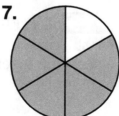

_____

8.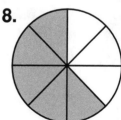

_____

Egg-Citing Fractions

Students will "crack up" over this fun fraction activity!

DIRECTIONS

In this activity, students will use counters to fill fractional parts of reproducible page 53 or an egg carton. There are two levels—one for students who are new to fractions and one for students who have had some experience with fractions. Before you begin, you may need to review the terms *numerator* and *denominator*.

Naming Fractions (Level 1) The denominator will stand for "how many holes altogether" and the numerator will stand for "how many holes to fill with counters." One counter goes in each hole. Have students fill the egg carton to represent fractions from $\frac{1}{12}$ to $\frac{12}{12}$ (in any order). Ask: Which fraction is the same as $\frac{1}{2}$? Which fraction is the same as 1? Remind students to empty the egg carton between fractions. Students will see the fractions more clearly if they fill the carton in the same order each time.

Equivalent Fractions (Level 2) The denominator will stand for "how many equal parts to divide the egg carton into" and the numerator will stand for "how many of those parts to fill with counters." Have students fill the egg carton to represent $\frac{1}{12}$, $\frac{1}{2}$, $\frac{3}{4}$, $\frac{2}{3}$, $\frac{6}{12}$, $\frac{2}{12}$, $\frac{1}{6}$, $\frac{8}{12}$, $\frac{9}{12}$, $\frac{12}{12}$, and $\frac{4}{12}$ (in any order). Ask: Which of these fractions are equivalent (different names for the same fraction)? How do you know?

ASSESSMENT

Have students record their work in words or pictures. Look for students who are transposing the numerator and denominator, and students are having trouble differentiating similar-looking fractions such as $\frac{1}{12}$ and $\frac{1}{2}$.

▶▶▶ EXTENSION

For students who are ready to go farther with fractions, attach two egg cartons together and challenge them to discover as many equivalent fractions as they can using all 24 cups ($\frac{4}{24} = \frac{2}{12} = \frac{1}{6}$, etc.).

Name _____

Egg-Citing Fractions

Ready, Set, Go!

This logic activity introduces students to sets and attributes.

DIRECTIONS

1. Display your set of classroom objects and invite students to make sets by grouping things that share common attributes (characteristics). Each set must have a name, such as things to write with, things we read, and so on.

2. Distribute reproducible page 55, the string, and scissors. Have students cut out the 16 pictures. They should also tie the two ends of their length of string into a knot and form the string into a circle on the floor or on a desktop.

3. Have students group some of the 16 pictures inside the circle to form a set. If students need help forming sets, ask them the following questions: What shape is it? What is it used for? What is it made from? What size is it? Who would use it? When a set is complete, students will record the name of the set and the objects in it on a sheet of paper. Then they can go on to form new sets. Here are some sample sets:

Things with holes: cheese, cup, button, cracker, sneaker, ring.

Things you can eat: orange, cheese, cracker, pizza.

ASSESSMENT

Look for students who are using faulty rules for their sets, such as things that I have seen. (This type of rule describes a relationship to the objects, rather than the attributes of the objects themselves. The rule would also be impossible for someone else to follow.)

▶▶▶ EXTENSION

◆ Suggest that students find extra photos (cut from magazines) or have them draw their own pictures, either to fit existing categories or to form new categories.

◆ With a second circle of string, students can create a Venn diagram. Show students how to to use it when an object shares two attributes (for example, it's round and you can eat it).

Name_____

Ready, Set, Go!

Cut out the pictures. What things can go together?
Make sets!

Logic Sandwiches

Here's a tasty introduction to logical thinking—creating silly sandwich combinations.

Grouping

Small groups

You'll Need

◆ Drawing paper
◆ Crayons
◆ Scissors
◆ Paper
◆ Pencils

PREPARATIONS

Write the list of sandwich ingredients on the chalkboard.

Two slices of bread
Peanut butter
Pickles
Swiss cheese
Bubble gum
Ketchup

DIRECTIONS

1. Draw attention to the list of sandwich ingredients. With three ingredients between two pieces of bread, how many different combinations do students think can be made? Ask them to guess. Then divide your class into groups, distribute drawing paper, crayons, and scissors, and have group members draw and cut out the ingredients. With sandwich fixings in hand, they can find out how many combinations are really possible!

2. Now have each group use the cutouts to create as many three-filling sandwiches as possible—no matter how unusual! They can create the sandwiches by placing different combinations of fillings between the two slices of bread. Any order is fine, but changing the order of ingredients does not change the sandwich. Pickles, Swiss cheese, and ketchup is the same as Swiss cheese, ketchup, and pickles.

3. Have students record their findings. They might make a list or draw a picture of each sandwich. When all groups think they have exhausted the possible combinations, discuss students' findings. There are ten possible three-filling combinations—did any group find all of them?

ASSESSMENT

Look for groups that are using some kind of organizational strategy in order to find and record new combinations and to avoid repeating ones they've already made.

➤➤➤ EXTENSION

If students have found all of the three-filling combinations, have them form two-filling combinations (ten possibilities) and four-filling combinations (five possibilities). Or add one more filling (how about spinach?) and continue the three-filling search (20 possibilities).

Put the Brakes on Math Mistakes!

Students find and correct math mistakes.

DIRECTIONS

1. Store owner Bob needs some help with the signs in his store window. Tell students they'll be looking for math mistakes to help him fix the signs. Discuss the kinds of mistakes that can occur with numbers. When is it important not to make math mistakes?

2. Distribute reproducible page 58 and challenge students to find and correct the mistakes. You may want to tell them there are 8 mistakes on the signs, and one more that isn't a sign.

3. When students have made their corrections, have volunteers share their ideas. Talk about the numbers they've suggested to fix Bob's signs. Do students all have the same answers? Is more than one answer reasonable/possible?

ASSESSMENT

Check that students have found all of the mistakes and that they have fixed the mistakes with reasonable corrections. **Mistakes:** 8 days a week should be 7; 8:75 PM is not possible; $10.99 off mountain bikes; bicycle chain is $6.00 a foot; bike helmets are $14.99; you save only $.01, not $1.00, on 2 rolls of tape; free stickers can't be 10 cents each; half-price bicycle seats should be $8.50. The additional mistake—a clock with three hands.

➡➡➡ EXTENSION

Ask students to find examples of real-life math mistakes. They might look in the newspaper, on menus in restaurants, on signs in store windows. Make a collection and post it on a classroom bulletin board.

Grouping

Individual

You'll Need

◆ **Put the Brakes on Math Mistakes (reproducible page 58),** one copy for each student
◆ Pencils

Writing Connection

Ask students to address the following question on a sheet of paper or in their math journals: What are some of the problems that math mistakes could cause people?

Put the Brakes on Math Mistakes!

Take a look at the signs on Bob's store.
Circle any mistake you see. Then fix the
mistake so that the sign is correct.

BOB'S BIKE BARN

Bike
Helmets
$14. 999

OPEN
9:30AM-8:75PM

OPEN
8 DAYS
A WEEK

* SALE *
$10 off selected
Mountain Bikes
Were $139.99
Now $129.00

Handlebar Tape
$3.99 a roll
Buy two for $7.99
SAVE $1.00

Bicycle Baskets
$12.99 each
Two for $25.00
SAVE $.98

* FREE *
Bicycle
Stickers
$.10 each

Bicycle Chain
$.50 an inch
That's only $5.00 a foot

½ off all
Bicycle Seats
Were $17.00
Now $9.50

Problems and More

Put on your thinking cap to solve these problems!

1. HOW MANY STUDENTS?

Estimate the number of students in your school. How did you do it?

_____

_____

_____

2. UPSIDE DOWN

What two-digit number reads the same upside down as it does right side up?

_____

3. CATS IN LINE

One cat walked in front of two cats. One cat walked behind two cats. One cat walked between two cats. How many cats were there? (Hint: Draw a picture!)

_____

4. NUMBER PATTERN

Here are the first five figures in a pattern. Draw the next figure.

5. CUTTING THE CAKE!

What is the fewest number of cuts you could make in order to cut a cake into six slices? (Hint: Draw a picture!)

_____

Problems and More

6. MISSING INFORMATION

Write the information you'd need to solve each of these problems.

◆ A cheese sandwich costs 80 cents more than a glass of juice. How much do they cost altogether?

◆ One gallon of paint will cover 1,200 square feet. How many gallons does Ruby need to paint her kitchen?

◆ Margo has $5. Can she buy a new notebook and a box of pencils?

7. TIME OUT!

Tessa started her homework at 4:30. She finished 45 minutes later. What time did Tessa finish her homework? How did you figure it out?

_____

8. MILK MONEY

A half gallon of milk costs $1.28. Ms. Cowper has 2 quarters, 5 dimes, and 3 nickels. Does she have enough money to buy the milk?

_____

9. PLENTY OF PATTERNS

Figure out each pattern. Then complete it.

5, 10, 15, 20, ___, ___, ___, ___

2, 4, 9, 16, 25, ___, ___, ___, ___

1, 2, 3, 5, 8, 13, 21 ___, ___, ___, ___

10. HOW MANY NUMBERS

Use the digits 5, 7, and 3. Write all the three-digit numbers you can make.

_____

_____

_____

_____

_____

_____

Answers on page 64.

An Assessment Toolkit

Alternative methods of assessment provide a comprehensive profile for each student. As students work on their activities in *Brain-Boosting Math Activities*, here are some ways you might observe and record their work. Alone or in combination, they can provide a quick snapshot that adds to your knowledge of students' development in mathematics. They also give you concrete observations to share with families at reporting time.

FILE CARDS

An alphabetical file system, with a card for each student, provides a handy way to keep notes on students' progress. Choose a few students each day that you plan to observe. Pull their cards, jot down the date and activity, and record comments about their work.

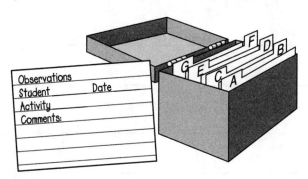

CLIPBOARDS

With a list of students attached to your clipboard, you can easily move about the classroom and jot down observations about their work and their thinking. If you want to focus on a particular skill or competency, you can create a quick checklist and simply check as you observe.

STICKY NOTES

As you circulate while individuals or small groups are working, create a sticky note for students who show particular strengths or areas for your attention and help. Be sure to date the note. The advantage to this technique is that you can move the notes to a record folder to create a profile; you can also cluster students with similar competencies as a reminder for later grouping.

CHECKLISTS AND RUBRICS

We've given you a few ready-made checklists and rubrics for assessment ideas. You can use them, or modify them to suit your own needs. Invite students to assess their own work—they are honest and insightful, and you'll have another perspective on their mathematical development!

Name _____ Date _____

Self-Evaluation Form

ACTIVITY _____

1. The activity was **(HARD   EASY)** to complete because _____

_____

_____

2. The part of the activity I did best was _____

_____

_____

3. I could have done a better job if _____

_____

4. The mathematics I used was _____

_____

5. After completing the activity I felt _____

because _____

_____

6. I would rate my work on the activity as **(EXCELLENT GOOD FAIR POOR)**

because _____

_____

_____

Evaluation Checklist

Activity _____ Date _____ Group _____

Students					
MATHEMATICS KNOWLEDGE					
Understands problem or task					
Formulates and carries out a plan					
Explains concepts clearly					
Uses models or tools appropriately					
Makes connections to similar problems					
Can create similar problems					
MATHEMATICAL PROCESSES					
Justifies responses logically					
Listens carefully to others and evaluates information					
Reflects on and explains procedures					
LEARNING DISPOSITIONS					
Tackles difficult tasks					
Perseveres					
Shows confidence in own ability					
Collaborates/shares ideas					

SCORING RUBRIC

3 Fully accomplishes the task

Shows full understanding of the central mathematical idea(s)

Communicates thinking clearly using oral explanation or written, symbolic, or visual means

2 Partially accomplishes the task

Shows partial understanding of the central mathematical idea(s)

Written or oral explanation partially communicates thinking, but may be incomplete, misdirected, or not clearly presented

1 Does not accomplish the task

Shows little or no grasp of the central mathematical idea(s)

Recorded work or oral explanation is fragmented and not understandable

Answers to Problems and More

PAGES 34-35

1. 360 x 1; 180 x 2; 120 x 3; 90 x 4; 72 x 5; 60 x 6; 45 x 8; 40 x 9; 36 x 10; 30 x 12; 24 x 15; 18 x 20

2. $4.96

3.

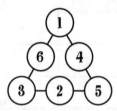

4. One penny, one nickel, one dime, and one quarter make 41 cents. You can add one nickel and 4 pennies, or 9 pennies, to get 50 cents.

5. 5 + 4 − 9 + 3 + 2 − 1 = 4

6. 13 triangles:
9 small (interior)
3 medium (interior)
1 large (the entire triangle)

7.

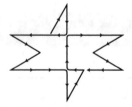

8.

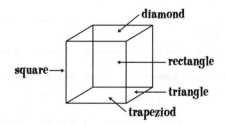

9. $\frac{1}{2}$ of $\frac{1}{2}$ is $\frac{1}{4}$.

10. Answers will vary.

PAGES 59-60

1. Answers will vary. Students may take an average class size of 30 students and multiply 30 by the number of classes in the school.

2. Answers include 11, 88, 69, and 96.

3. 3 cats

4.

5. three cuts

6. You would have to know:
♦ how much either the cheese sandwich or the glass of juice costs
♦ how many square feet Ruby's kitchen measures
♦ how much a notebook costs; how much a box of pencils costs

7. She finished at 5:15.

8. No. She has only $1.15.

9. 25, 30, 35, 40 (skip-count by 5s); 36, 49, 64, 81 (consecutive square numbers); 34, 55, 89, 144 (sums of the preceding two numbers)

10. 573; 735; 357; 375; 753; 537